THE BURNING PAGES

THE BURNING PAGES

BY

CECILIA KNIGHT

2024

The Burning Pages
Copyright © 2024 by Cecilia Knight.

All rights reserved. This book or any portion thereof may not be reproduced or used in any manner whatsoever without the express written permission of the author except for the use of brief quotations in the context of reviews.

ISBN: 979-8-218-47064-7

Cover design by Rachel Clift.
Book design & layout by Rachel Clift.
rcliftpoetry.com

First printing edition, 2024.

@ceciliaknightpoems
ceciliaknight.com
Cecilia Knight

There's nothing to fear here.

xoxo – CK

POEMS

i'd like to say, if you were here
you'd be proud of the woman i've become
but i don't think that's true
i think you'd be disappointed
because i kissed a black guy once
and a Mexican
and a woman
and i say the word *fuck* a lot
and i hate wearing dresses
and i have 11 tattoos
and a very life-like dildo
that glows in the dark
and i like big cities
and rap music
and spicy food
and i don't go to church
and i'm high as i write this
so i don't think you'd actually like me

i think i'm cool as fuck though

GOODBYE
after Chelsie Diane

goodbye to my 20s
goodbye to the people pleaser
pleasing people that will never be pleased
goodbye covering my tattoos so my dad doesn't see
goodbye speaking to people who don't listen
goodbye gray floors
gray cubicle walls
bright red bathroom stalls
old men with no balls
goodbye corporate America
GOOD
BYE
what a waste of my fucking life
goodbye filtering my Instagram posts because
what. if. they. see?
good –
they'll see the real me

goodbye to the holes in my socks and
sc ar ci ty
thoughts
goodbye red
goodbye yellow
i need my house to be more mellow
goodbye expensive store bought herbs
i'm growing my own
goodbye saying yes when i mean no

goodbye being afraid to grow
and never letting my feelings show
goodbye perfectly straight hair
goodbye you shouldn't have hair there
goodbye waxing – i genuinely don't care!
goodbye pretending i'm fine
goodbye grocery lines
goodbye to anyone and anything wasting my time
goodbye to this pen that doesn't write
goodbye missing my flight
goodbye dimming my light
goodbye socially acceptable responses
you
will
hear
my truth
goodbye house hunting –
i don't want to move!
goodbye convincing –
you're the one that will lose
goodbye book club
and reading books i'd never choose
goodbye asking permission
goodbye apologizing for good decisions
goodbye prison sentence
goodbye
goodbye
goodbye

Love Letter #1

look at her
let your eyes dance down the curves of her legs
i don't much care for feet
but i could stare at hers all day
she takes care of herself
manicured hands
beautiful hair
it's bigger now
just like her

i bet you didn't know she speaks Spanish
she freezes when the waiter comes to take our order
she doesn't like the way her accent sounds
but her body knows that language
when the bachata drums start to play
she's fluent again
like it never left

i bet you didn't know how open minded she is
she loves hearing about weird interests
when you let her in like that, she softens
she's forgiving
kind
full of love
spark and desire
like he never left

she listens to the same songs over and over again
can belt out an entire Lorde album during a shower
without missing a word
water as hot as her
i can't see myself in the mirror

THE BURNING PAGES

don't need to

she has a soft spot for animals
and wants to heal the world
her dreams are so big
bigger than the moon
speaking of the moon
don't get her started on the moon

don't let her cook for you
if you hate spicy food
she loves habanero and
Indian, Mexican, Italian too
always has dark chocolate nearby
eats pickles like popcorn
who does that?

she's got a thing for words
can't pick a movie to save her life
she likes period pieces and mysteries
mysteries in her dark eyes
god i hope
no i pray
my daughter has those eyes
the sound of her laughter
and how she dances in the kitchen
and loves with all that she is
makes me want to marry her
elope to the coast or an island

somewhere with water
somewhere with water

oh god
my thoughts are running wild tonight

oh god
i want your hand around my neck
tight

oh god
i want your lips on mine
either set is fine

OH GOD

my nails making stripes
up your back
i'm arching mine

ohgodohgodohgod

you say i'm doing it just right

my god

i can't stop trembling
oh
god

i must be ovulating

NO MEANS NO

when a man says *no* it's
out of the question
when a woman says *no* it's
maybe she can be convinced
no is the easiest word in the English language to
understand
so why is it so damn hard for a man?
if i say it differently, will it get through your thick
head?
fuck no!
god no!
please no!
should i type it in all caps?
or sign it with my hands?
tattoo it across my forehead?
unless i'm kicking and screaming
i must be teasing
and they will go on believing
that i am a waste of time
a woman can never make up her mind
r-e-s-p-e-c-t
apparently that doesn't apply to me
they want me to be a good girl and put on a show
but i will never stop screaming
NO
MEANS
FUCKING
NO

i think i'm dying

my head hurts
but it feels a little different this time
and the doctors say i'm totally fine
my chest hurts, i can't breathe
is it a panic attack or a heart attack?
the signs are the same
why does my mole look like that?
my fingers are achy
i'm too young for arthritis though
aren't i?
why does my throat hurt?
is it covid or just allergies?
TikTok says i have parasites
i think
i'm dying

THE BURNING PAGES

i'm sorry for poking at your stomach
when i know you're self conscious about it

i'm sorry for chastising you for loving so hard
and for gaslighting you when you said
something didn't feel right

i'm sorry for saying your dreams were too big
and for saying
maybe next time
when i knew there wouldn't be a next time

i'm sorry for planning the perfect 3 month trip through Europe
and then not getting on that flight

i should've stood up for you
when i heard them call you names
and i should've encouraged you to love freely
while you still had it in you
i should've listened when you begged me not to trust him
i should've let you show me the world through your eyes

i should've written those poems with you
and taken those pictures with you
and made those videos with you
and taken that class with you
and shared my soul with you

i should've gotten on that fucking flight

MAKE ME

it takes a lot more than
money and a pretty face
to grab my attention

you must have forgotten
who i am

you want me to call you daddy
how about you make me

People Pleaser

a people pleaser, if you please
will it make you happy, to see me bleed?
heart on a silver platter, just for you
i'll even make it pretty, if you need me to
gold medal gymnast, bending til i break
and i break
break
broken
lying on the floor, but you're needing more
my chest is open, my legs are broken
slipped on my own blood
you didn't catch me, or even notice the
tiny little spark i hid in my locket
just in case you decided to take
a little more, but you got bored
and left me naked by the door
alone
empty
cold

Questions for my exes

do you still fart in your sleep?
oh wait that wasn't very ladylike of me
are you threatened by my masculine energy?
what about my sexuality or femininity?
you were always threatened by a lot
i hope you sit in that apartment and rot

and then there's the guy who was the high school mascot
what was his name?
damn
i forgot

hey T
does your wife know that you slept with me?
does she know you chased me through the parking lot
cursing and screaming?
does she know you stalk my IG story?
and that your daughter's name
is the name you stole from me?
when you look at that baby
do you think of me?

I AM DADDY

and my babygirl deserves
a sweet treat every day of the week
a tub filled with bath salts and flower petals
purple flowers in every room of the house
a special edition record from her favorite artist
two weeks in France sipping wine in the country-
side
my babygirl deserves to have her nails done
pizza? at midnight?
you got it
another book for the overflowing collection?
how about two, or three?
my love for her is free
she deserves my attention
she deserves grace
she deserves peace

Aesop

did you just
puke on my pillow?
yesterday you got your face stuck
in a cup of water you were drinking out of because the
four water bowls you have aren't good enough
and the day before that you snagged my brand new
blanket
i've only used once
but damn you're fucking cute
and somehow you know exactly when i need you to
come purr on my chest
i want to record your voice and use it as my text-tone
i'm glad you exist

Love Letter #2

i'm not ready to leave
four years have felt like seconds
i dusted you off and made you my own
and that love was reciprocated
your strong old bones held me tight
kept me safe while i cried
watched me become a wife
fusing together over the years
our souls intertwined

to leave you for another has my gut wrenching
tornadoes in my heart

and you say, *go. it's time.*

i will hold you close until the day i die
your photo hidden in my locket
i will keep you like a love letter
creased and crinkled

i hope the next one treats you well
patches up the holes i made
keeps the ghosts at bay
and i hope she stays

WITCH

i'm so sick of the trends
the, i'm so small,
need validation from men
i'm literally just a girl
girl you better drop that shit
can't stand that stupid bit
women have so much power
i wish they'd realize it
the men know it
why do you think they burned us?
why do you think they fear us?
hate us?
belittle us?
maim us?
if i were in Salem
they would tie me to a stake made of oak
the same as my last name
my father's name
set me ablaze
i am made from the ashes of those who burned before me
and the burning stops with me
my daughter will. be. free.

there is always madness in love

always. bad kind and good kind. mad because they left their dishes in the sink. mad because they have 43 tabs open on the computer. mad for no reason. mad because they look good in all black. mad because the way they whisper in your ear sends chills down your spine. mad because you'd cross oceans for them. mad because they see you. *really* see you.

i want you to wreck me
utterly destroy me
but not in a way that breaks my heart
and crushes my soul
no

shake me to my core
and make me question everything

wake up!
you've been sleeping,
not living!
you deserve the world,
it's yours for the taking!
your fire isn't burning bright enough today!

that's the kind of wreckage i crave
the kind that turns my spark into a forest fire
the kind that inspires intensity
i want to get drunk on you
look at my craziest ideas
and tell me they're not wild enough

you're thinking small again!
open up that beautiful mind!
you're seeing in black and white!
read between the lines!
turn the book upside down,
fold the page,
read it backwards!

move me

when you do that to me

THE BURNING PAGES

i'm so soft for you
on my knees for you
so hot for you
burning so bright
and wildly for you
would burn the entire world
for you
keep you warm for eternity
anything and everything
for you
only you

what you must know is that
i am never boring
my darling
when a feeling comes i let it
devour my every bone
i was not made for restraint
when i love
when i grieve
the euphoria
the despair
i eat it entirely
i cry and love and tremble and scream
you would not have me any other way
and
neither
would
i
i will not
tone myself down to fit in a mold
this sickness you say i have is
a gift
i am nothing if not bold
i say way too much
much too early
and through my intensity
the glass breaks eventually
so no
i will not hold back
nor will i hide
to do that is to die
could i?
settle for less?
less than a fire
less than i desire

yes.
i could.
but
i
will
not.

i will not let myself rot in a love that is lacking.

you're so hot
after Chelsie Diane

you're so hot
i want to rub the finest oil on your feet
and then lick it off of them

you're so hot
i want to trace with my fingers
every inch of your body
the curve of your breasts
the bone of your hip
those supple lips

you're so hot
i want my mouth filled with your poofy hair
i want to find your dark poofy hair everywhere
in my sock
in my underwear

you're so hot
hotter than candle wax
dripping slowly down the side
pooling on the wooden mantle
enticing

you're so hot
i want to take your picture
blow it up
hang it in a gallery
hang it in the Louvre
a permanent place

Explore Page

you're so hot
i want to quit my job
sell my house
and buy a one way ticket to Italy
just because you said you like pasta

you're so hot
i could listen to your favorite song on repeat
your favorite artists on repeat

you're so hot
i could listen to you sing
every
single
Lorde and Taylor Swift song
forever and ever

you're so hot
i write pages and pages of you in my journal
my hand is cramping
my pens are out of ink
I NEED A NEW JOURNAL

you're so hot

i'm scared and turned on at the same time

you're so hot
i stalk your instagram daily

i'm touching myself in public
i hope the old lady over there doesn't see
let her see
LET THE WORLD SEE
INDESCRIBABLE
B-E-A-UTY
you're so hot
i'm moaning on the subway train

HOT
HOT
HOT

House on Fire

how did i not know our house was on fire?
i couldn't sense the heat or smell the smoke
i knew i couldn't breathe, i just didn't know why
call 911 but no one picks up, i'm frantic
why didn't you wake me
when you noticed the flames?
a fire can't put itself out
i'm suffocating now
you're opening the windows
thank you for trying
but all you're doing
is fueling the danger that is brewing
a blaze left untamed will consume everything in its path
we need to get out
before it's too late

perhaps it's already too late

ADHD

shit
i walked out of the kitchen
and forgot to close the cabinet
now the cat is asleep inside of it
on top of the plates

i had a thought
which bounced off another
and another
and suddenly i can't find
any of them

i did laundry today
and found clothes in the dryer from a week ago
my half eaten breakfast is still sitting on the table
it's cold
i swear i just took it off the stove
5 minutes ago

i have 3 songs stuck in my head at once
and simultaneously being haunted by something i said
to someone
in December of 2019

why hasn't he texted me back?
i responded in my head
but maybe i never hit send
or maybe he hates me

i'm really thirsty
got out of bed, walked into the kitchen
pet the cat

THE BURNING PAGES

why is the neighbor outside so late?
i left my dinner bowl in the sink
better put that away
god i hate gnats
it's late, go back to bed
so warm, so cozy
i'm really thirsty
damnit
i forgot the water

i've seen grown adults laugh at someone for playing D&D
why do your hobbies make you better than me?
the thought of tapping a ball into a hole
makes me want to die but
i think you should do that if
it makes you feel alive
let me have my avocado toast
you can still have pumpkin spice
let me have my Halloween decorations
and you can have your Christmas lights
i'll dress in all black
while you wear only pink and white
and that will be alright because
it makes us happy
so just let us be and live our lives

Girlfriends

let me tell you a secret
i want us to be girlfriends
wait, i mean, girl friends
it's the way you cover your face when you giggle
and how your eyes light up when you talk about Asheville
for a moment, let's pretend he doesn't exist
i'll take you to get your nails done
don't worry, i'll grab matcha on the way
i'll help you sort through the colors
(but we both know which ones you'll choose)
we can go thrifting
i'll take you to the vegan place
then we can watch Practical Magic
and if it comes down to it,
i'll squish the bugs for you
(even though i'm secretly afraid of them too)
maybe we'll yell our hearts out to Paramore
and after we're done screaming,
we can hold hands under the full moon
i'll help you cast your spells
and pick tiny flowers for your hair
because i think that's what girl friends do
but it's my little secret
one i will never tell

Home

it's the sound of the *Survivor* theme song
it's the smell of coffee in the morning
it's *Sonic* and *Baskin Robbins* after school
it's homegrown tomatoes and peppers
it's cucumbers with too much salt
it's a pot of chili in the Fall
it's *Velveeta* and *Rotel* and *Tostitos*
it's macaroni and cheese
or a grilled cheese sandwich
it's a lot of cheese and *Goldfish*
it's cold bricks and scored concrete under my feet
so i wear fuzzy socks
it's the pitter patter of a tiny dog
it's staying up late dressing up as pirates
and chasing clowns
it's *pull my finger*
it's fireworks in the cul-de-sac
it's choreographed dances to songs we don't understand
it's falling asleep on pontoon boats
and fighting off the Arkansas mosquitos
it's Easter eggs with money inside
it's chasing lightning bugs at night
it's *i bought another lottery ticket – i think i might win this time!*
it's *i love you*
and *i'm sorry*
and *it's fine*

i'm bi, by the way
it's such a forward thing to say
but how else am i supposed to find a pretty girl to kiss?
don't worry, dad
i'll end up with a dude anyway
i still want that kiss

Chill TF Out

i wasn't made for this life
i long for something more
more than a box to check
a check to collect
and every goddamn email is important
life altering
MUST RESPOND NOW
before another one comes in
ding
ding
ding
goes the washing machine
a dryer that can sing
but can't dry clothes
i can hear its song in my sleep
the anthem to the movie of emails i haven't opened yet
you don't want to see that in theaters
trust me
streams daily in my house
wait until the part where the cats forget what time it is
dinner at 6:30
but it's 6:05
FEED ME NOW OR I'LL CLAW OUT MY SISTER'S EYES
the best creativity happens at night
and i spend it recovering from my life

chamomile lavender tea so i chill the fuck out
marijuana leaves in my tea so i chill the fuck out
A LITTLE MARY JANE SO I CHILL THE FUCK OUT
too much and i fall asleep on the couch

THE BURNING PAGES

a pen in my hand instead of a mouse
a camera in my hand instead of a mouse
ANYTHING IN MY HAND INSTEAD OF A MOUSE
i'm so fucking tired of this pretty little mouse

a pen in my hand so i get it all out
get it all out
CRY
SCREAM
SHOUT
do you see what i see?
the wind and the willow tree
and the life that is meant for me
must be
will be
is

we have a habit of only seeing what we want to see
like everything is okay even though i fall asleep
at 8:30
like a large house for our family and not the mold on
the ceiling
like not seeing the man down the street who months
later would terrorize me
like not seeing that money does not equal happy
and fun does not equal love
like not seeing how empty i feel
and thinking that emotions are no big deal
like seeing what we are told to see –
a job, a house, a car, a family
we have a habit of only thinking logically
and i think
that
was the death of me

Diwali

i frightened you
shivered at my touch
scarred by someone else
forced to trust a stranger

i gave you your space
i was gentle
day by day
i saw the fear in your eyes
transform to love

the mother bear in you
brought out the mother bear in me
roaring

you became my shadow
inseparable
you dance with me in the kitchen now
my favorite walking partner
all dressed up for Halloween
we check the mail together
inspecting it carefully

i did not know i was capable
of such a love

i would burn my house for you

and when the time comes
for you to cross the rainbow
they will have to
rip. me.
from your side

Nothing Boys

this poem came to me in a dream
it's sad how the boys i've loved
still haunt me in my sleep

i'm sick and tired of these Nothing Boys
you know the ones
they treat women like toys

i wrote a song when i was seventeen
asked the guy i was dating to write me a guitar piece
something fancy
it was awesome
coolest thing i'd ever heard
he stole it from *Switchfoot*
i pity the woman he's married to now
i bet he's bad in bed

do you know a *Nothing Man?*
beer belly Stan
never grew up
in a 50 something year old boy band
i call them Nothing Boys
because they're not real men
and that's what they add to your life:
nothing

they might be pretty
but pretty fades
and true beauty doesn't lie in the face
so don't let them get in the way

don't choose the boy who listens to the depths of your
heart
and responds with nothing
choose the one who drives five hours to take you to
the audition of your dreams
those are the boys suited for queens
you deserve so much more than sweet
nothings

people walking people talking people watching
people smiling people crying people spiraling
people i like admiring
people dancing people romancing people expanding
people i want to know
people loving people hugging people trusting
people eating people reading people feeling
people people-ing
people with trendy clothes and cringey jokes
people with joy in their eyes sparkling in the lights
people i will keep alive forever
in the pages i will write and
the photos i will capture
from the pov of a wallflower

the men before you
who crawled on their knees before me
it's because of them i raised the bar
so incredibly high
if my soul does not recognize
you as a contender
you will never get the keys
to the palace gates
my kingdom is reserved
for the very few who
can match my intensity
and fear not of my deep seas
my heart belongs to a man
with an eye patch and black beard
he worships my waters and
does not try to restrain my waves
this is the man that holds the key
a man who recognizes his queen
so do not try to scale these walls
my cannons are ready
this queen has needs and
you
will
not
change
me

Happy Birthday

i woke up in a bad mood today
wanting to scream and cry
and throw everything in sight
i finally realize why

today is your birthday

i remember asking you when it was
i already had the perfect gift in mind
you didn't ask the same question in return
and i didn't notice at the time
there were a lot of things i didn't notice back then
like how you sometimes made me feel disregarded
even though i held you in the utmost importance
you came across so gentle, innocent, selfless
so i put you on a pedestal
high up in the clouds

i will never do that again

happy birthday
can you hear me all the way up there?
happy birthday
from the girl who just wanted you to care
happy birthday
i really thought what we had was rare

happy birthday

intermission

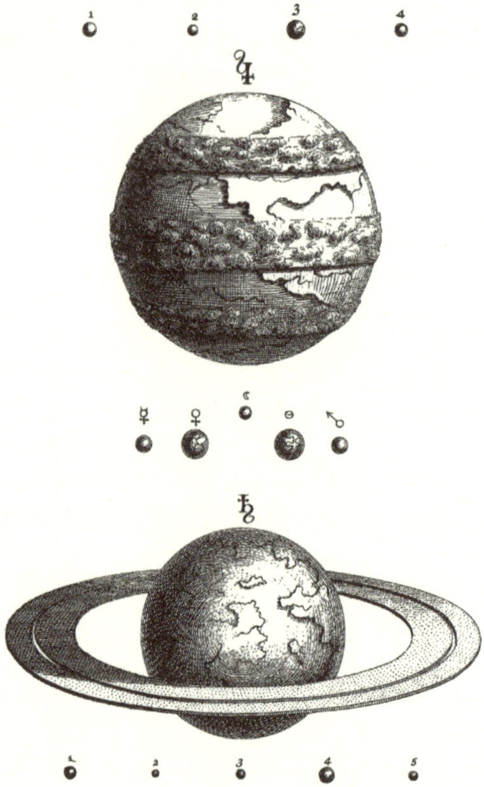

1 2 3 4
♃
☿ ♀ ☾ ⊕ ♂
♄
1 2 3 4 5

Saturn has returned
and she's ready for battle

when you see me now, you're probably confused

yes i have tattoos
and different religious views
yes i've learned to recognize abuse
and am no longer amused
by lame shitty dudes!

and i know you're watching me

watch me tell all the men
to suck. my. dick.
watch me piss off the republicans
lifting up the gays girlies and children
because *they* are what purity *actually* looks like
safe
kind
heaven sent

watch me dance with my middle finger up
watch me dance – i'm no longer stuck!
watch me dance while you stay in your rut

when you see me now, you're probably confused

remember when you tried to mold me?
so i could be useful to you?

remember when you tried to silence my truth?

i bet now
when you look at me
you're confused

and i bet your big ass ego is bruised

THE BURNING PAGES

women
there's a reason why men have always tried
to keep us caged
our bodies go through phases and seasons like the
moon like mother nature
we grow human lives inside our
not so fragile bodies

women
have
power

and inside every one of us is
a Cleopatra, a Queen
creator, CEO
beauty AND beast

WOMEN

we grow our own wings
we set ourselves free

WOMAN

listen to me

do not let
his scarcity mindset
limited way of thinking
lack of depth
make you feel inept

get up

hop on one leg
crawl if you have to

reclaim your sky

do not let your soul die

you. must. *fly*.

Love Letter #3

dear fisheye lens
i'm obsessed with the way you view the world
longing to see through your eyes
how i crave the beautiful distortion
i need my hands on you
now
no better feeling than my hand
wrapped
around your throat

but please don't tell my pen –
she will go into a jealous frenzy

poetry does not like to share

little does she know
she had my heart first
you may have my eyes
but she has my soul
i hope you don't mind

i'm way too hot for this shit

too tight
push up bras
eye rolls from your grandma
lukewarm food
sugary booze
corporate dudes
ice cold
sticky
gas station pumps
watered down lattes
too old to be acting this way
never been to therapy
no good punks
stupid situationships
apologizing for my opinions
being put in a box
being put on your clock
misogynistic jokes that aren't funny
honey honey
listen –
i'm way too hot for this shit

i want to kiss you, but like *really* kiss you
what i mean is,
i want you to lift me up and set me on your lap
my body burns for you
i want you to reach deep into my soul
take my breath away
make me scream your name
the lightning outside is weak
compared to how i'd feel with you inside
kiss me softly, grip me tightly
command me with your eyes
consume all of me, spill out of me
make me feel like i have died
and entered an alternate universe
that even god himself couldn't have created
i want to kiss you

OOPS I DID IT AGAIN
after Britney Spears

i'm not that innocent
if you open the drawer next to my bed
you'll find my weed stash and sex toys
instead of a Bible
i guess you can say i'm a rebel now
but i don't really care for that title
missed the rebellious teenage years
locked in a cage
now i'm late to the party
pissing off the patriarchy
that is just so typically me
OOPS I DID IT AGAIN
got two more tattoos
just another thing they didn't want me to do
you can't say that
you can't wear those
you can't talk to them
it's no wonder i have no friends
oh baby baby
i'm the only person i will be pleasing today
my angel wings have been detached
i've traded my halo for a pitchfork
i'm not that innocent

i never understood religions and all the rules they've made up
like banning everything they're afraid of

Eden might have been a garden
but it was also a prison
what kind of god keeps its children in a cage?
why do you think the church tries to keep women off stage?
why do you think the government is taking books from our kids?

it wasn't the fruit that was off limits

it was the independence
it was the knowledge
it was the freedom

i sometimes wonder what would happen if you left
i would miss the sound of your keys and laughing
with your family
loving me unconditionally despite my selfish tendencies
and making me laugh so effortlessly
your ability to curate epic playlists and
the willingness to be my kitchen sidekick
i love you's disguised as insults and encouraging my
every impulse
i'd miss the long drives at night and all the purple
lights
your daughters i've adopted as my own and
the safety of a home in which i don't have to pretend
i'd miss my best friend and our trips overseas
so don't go
please

different shades of beige

i was raised to be a suburban mom
you know the one
tan dress pants
brown Louis Vuitton bag
different shades of beige
makes cupcakes for the class
head of the PTA
perfectly mowed grass
monogram on the back of a Mercedes
but god had other plans for me
she knew that life would not satisfy
she knew
thank god she knew

i woke up with your name written on my skin
how did it get there? did you write it?
i washed it off, it floated into the air
it echoes in my ear
is that you? are you here?
i hold it in my hands
tracing each letter with my fingers
in my dreams, in my mind, it lingers
say it
say it
scream it
don't say it
haunting
consuming
all encompassing
that name

I want to feel it
after Isabella Dorta

i want to be texted first
i want poems written about me
and love letters given to me
i want pictures taken of me without having to ask
i want kisses in the rain
and unannounced visits on my lunch break
i want my coffee order to be memorized
i want sunrises on the beach
and emotion filled speech
i want dance parties in the kitchen
and singing in the car with the windows down
i want purple flowers because they're my favorite
i want to be sent a song because it made you think of me
and gentle touches on my back while i'm sleeping
i want late nights out and movie nights in
i want to be introduced to your friends
but most of all
i want to be chosen, over and over again
i want to be discovered, known, and understood
i want to feel loved unconditionally
i want to *feel* it

face down in a pillow
i can't breathe

head under water for a little too long
i can't breathe

pinned against the wall of an overly crowded elevator
i. can't. breathe.

falling from an airplane 14,000 feet up at 120mph
I CAN'T BREATHE

fire needs oxygen to grow

maybe that's why i'm dying

your wind isn't strong enough
to move my flames

Worth it

i only wear baggy sweatshirts
black lace under my baggy sweatshirts
nothing under my baggy sweatshirts
rosé in my left hand
smut in my right
not a man in sight
my kind of night
with a cat in my lap

i may dress in all black
but baby i eat in color
grow my own food in the summer
hot curry on the stove
i'm a bit of a witch i suppose

intelligence
love
magic
grace
a woman that takes up space
the type of beauty time won't erase
one of a kind soul that can't be replaced
trust me honey i'm worth the chase

my hydrangea bushes are flirting with me
what color will you be?
purple blue or pink?
they know what colors i long to see
i hear them snickering as i count their buds
taunting me as they dance in the sunlight
i walk past them and swear i can see them through the window
waving at me with their leaves
begging me to lay my cold naked body beneath them and dream

what color will you be?
what color will you be?
what color will you be?

Savage

i remember when you told me you were joining the Navy
i loved you for it
i hated you for it
our late night talks in the *Sonic* parking lot
early morning talks in the school parking lot
hidden texts during study hall
turned into letters from overseas
and photos of the beautiful places you went
we reconnected
every time you came back
except for the last time
i still tell you happy birthday
every year on Facebook
i got a new neighbor in 2022
with the same last name as you
hoped the two of you were related
prayed you were related
you're not
i still think of you every time i see him
one day you will read this poem
and know just how much our friendship meant to me
and that i still think about it years later
and that if you called tomorrow
i'd answer

didn't you know i needed you?

a gas station in the middle of nowhere
you were hungry so we stopped
my boyfriend wouldn't quit texting
i don't remember what he said
but i do remember how you made me feel next
i ran to the bathroom to hide my tears
don't cry in public
they say
that's not how a lady behaves herself
i forgot to lock the door
you didn't knock
i need to wash my hands
you said
well, you washed them of me, didn't you?
maybe you didn't know what to say
women supporting women
i guess your generation was different
but i didn't need any specific words or phrases
i just needed something, anything
i just needed you

Loose Papers

i don't delete blurry photos anymore
because you said you liked the ones i showed you before
now i appreciate the little accidents in life
like a road being blocked so i turn down your street to catch the next light
i still think of you when it rains
and i'm starting to think that life won't be the same without you in it
because when i send silly videos to my story, Instagram still recommends you first
even though i unfollowed you a week ago
and when i see crumbled up receipts and gum wrappers in the bottom of my purse i don't see trash
i see loose papers
and i wonder how many notebooks you've bought since the last time we were together
and if you've written about me in any of them
or if i'm just another loose paper
that you didn't have a pocket for
and i wonder if it was windy that night

Nightmares

maybe tonight i can sleep
and my thoughts won't terrorize me
charlotte will stay in her web all night
and the shadow will put down the knife this time
and my mind won't be awake while my body is dead
and i won't feel a heavy weight on my bed
that isn't my own
and i won't reach for my phone
or the light because when i open my eyes
without my screams i can breathe
and i can actually believe
that i got sleep last night

order in the court
we hereby find the defendant guilty
of false allegations and defamation
let's consider the evidence, shall we?
look at the accused
he couldn't have done it
see his clean smile
pinstripes
shiny watch
no, not him
silly silly
you really really
should get a hold of yourself
when he said *i love you*
did you think he
actually meant it?
5 years
that is your sentence
so let the suffering commence
ha ha
haunted by every word
every touch
every sound
that place
that taste
that name
that'll teach you and keep you
from being a silly silly girl
in a man's world

fall
the *-ber* months
some call it
life in its purest form
when the air is chilly and light
the most beautiful color palette
makes me want to eat seasonal soups and
grilled cheese sandwiches
sip hot tea by a bonfire
eat s'mores
on a hay bale
wearing my favorite hoodie
watch movies
read books
write poetry
i want to make love and
be held tight
under a blanket
hibernate as nature intended

HELLO

hello to my thirties
the best years of my life
hello fighting with all of my might
hello purple door
and seeing my name in a store
94 cameras
113 microphones
today is the last time you will ever feel alone
hello to the most books i've ever read
listening more to my heart than to my head
hello to my intuition and
creation creation creation
hello living with passion
having a dream and making it happen
hello goddess
hello mother
hello lifting up each other
hello authenticity
and showing up as me with ease
hello to altering our family tree
hello to
it. ends. with. me.
hello making people uncomfortable
that's just what i do
hello to many more unhidden tattoos
hello expanded thoughts
hello to the car that i bought
hello having peace of mind
hello well spent time
hello strong voice

and knowing that i have a choice
hello learning from the past
hello creating my own path
hello making love last
hello
hello
hello

as i approach 30
i begin to wonder about my future
and if i meet the definition of success

i didn't climb the corporate ladder
i actively fought against it
i don't make six figures, but
i paid off my car
and don't have credit card debt
i also don't have all the answers i was sent to university
to learn

but i have discovered that
money isn't the thing i want to earn most
it's love and respect
i do know what excites me about life and
gets me out of bed in the morning
when i live with authenticity and create with love
i give myself the kind of happiness money cannot buy

and i've realized
the definition of success isn't found in a bank account
having a house isn't the same as having a home
being content isn't the same as being happy

so for me
the definition of success
is having the ability to live authentically
unapologetically
to be madly in love with yourself and with life
because this isn't practice
it's the only one we have

Milton Keynes UK
Ingram Content Group UK Ltd.
UKHW021811050824
446478UK00020B/184